NEWSMAKERS

POPE FRANCIS

Catholic Spiritual Leader

by Kris Woll

Content Consultant
Massimo Faggioli
Assistant Professor of Theology
University of Saint Thomas

Core Library

An Imprint of Abdo Publishing
www.abdopublishing.com

www.abdopublishing.com

Published by Abdo Publishing, a division of ABDO, PO Box 398166, Minneapolis, Minnesota 55439. Copyright © 2015 by Abdo Consulting Group, Inc. International copyrights reserved in all countries. No part of this book may be reproduced in any form without written permission from the publisher. Core Library™ is a trademark and logo of Abdo Publishing.

Printed in the United States of America, North Mankato, Minnesota
082014
012015

THIS BOOK CONTAINS RECYCLED MATERIALS

Cover Photo: Riccardo De Luca/AP Images
Interior Photos: Riccardo De Luca/AP Images, 1; Michael Kappeler/picture-alliance/dpa/AP Images, 4; Dmitry Lovetsky/AP Images, 7; Red Line Editorial, 8; Ivan Fernandez/AP Images, 10; El Salvador School/AP Images, 12; Eduardo Di Baia/AP Images, 14; Massimo Sambucetti/AP Images, 16; L'Osservatore Romano/AP Images, 18, 20, 26, 31, 39; Dorling Kindersley/DK Images, 23; Reed Saxon/AP Images, 29; Natacha Pisarenko/AP Images, 32; Marcio Fernandes/Estadao Conteudo/AP Images, 34, 45; Pablo Martinez Monsivais/AP Images, 37

Editor: Arnold Ringstad
Series Designer: Becky Daum

Library of Congress Control Number: 2014944217

Cataloging-in-Publication Data
Woll, Kris.
 Pope Francis: Catholic spiritual leader / Kris Woll.
   p. cm. -- (Newsmakers)
Includes bibliographical references and index.
ISBN 978-1-62403-644-6
1. Francis, Pope, 1936- --Juvenile literature. 2. Popes--Biography--Juvenile literature.
1.Title.
282/.092--dc23
[B]

                                                              2014944217

CONTENTS

CHAPTER ONE

FROM FAR AWAY

During the day on March 13, 2013, black smoke came from the chimney of the Sistine Chapel in Vatican City, Rome. Inside, Roman Catholic Church officials called cardinals gathered to elect a new pope. The pope is the leader of one of the world's biggest religions, the Catholic Church, with 1.2 billion members. The previous pope, Benedict XVI, had stepped down. The black smoke

Crowds watched and waited in Vatican City for the announcement of a new pope in March 2013.

told onlookers that the cardinals had not yet selected a new pope. Thousands of people had gathered outside the chapel in Saint Peter's Square.

It rained and grew dark. Then a puff of white smoke appeared from the small chimney. A pope had been chosen. The bells of Saint Peter's Basilica rang in celebration, and the crowd cheered. Finally the red curtains of the balcony above the square opened for the official announcement. "We have a pope!" Cardinal Jean-Louis Tauran exclaimed in Latin, announcing Pope Francis to the world.

In the weeks to come, many news stories would focus on Pope Francis's simple life. They would discuss how he differed from past popes. They would report on his teachings about helping the poor.

But that night, the new pope gave only a short speech. "My brother cardinals have chosen one who is from the other end of the world," he began. "But here I am."

The newly elected Pope Francis greeted massive crowds from the balcony of Saint Peter's Basilica.

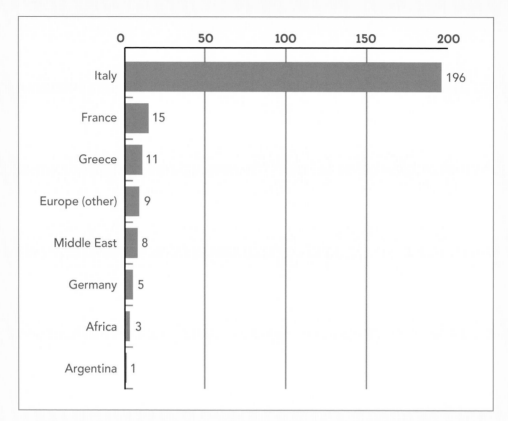

Where Have Popes Come From?
This chart shows where the popes have come from. What countries, continents, and regions have been home to the most popes? Why was Pope Francis so different from previous popes?

Growing Up in Argentina

Pope Francis's journey to Saint Peter's Square began in Buenos Aires, Argentina. He is the first pope in more than a thousand years who is not from Europe. He is also the first pope from Latin America.

Pope Francis was born with the name Jorge Mario Bergoglio on December 17, 1936, in Buenos Aires. Buenos Aires is the largest city in Argentina and is the nation's capital. In the late 1800s and early 1900s, it was a popular destination for immigrants from Europe. These people sought better opportunities and a new life. Jorge's grandparents on both sides immigrated to Argentina from Italy.

Jorge's father worked for a railroad company. His mother was a housewife. Jorge was the first-born child in his family. Four siblings would follow: Alberto, Oscar, Marta Regina, and Maria Elena. The Bergoglio

What Is Latin America?

Latin America is a term used to describe the countries in the Americas where the main language is Spanish, French, or Portuguese. These languages are based on the Latin language. They were brought to the Americas by Europeans hundreds of years ago. The country of Argentina sits at the bottom of Latin America. It is located on the southern end of South America.

Today the only remaining part of the house where Jorge grew up is the backyard.

family lived in the Flores neighborhood of Buenos Aires. Many of their neighbors were immigrants. Like the Bergoglios, many were Catholic.

Argentina is known for its love of tango and soccer. Jorge enjoyed both while growing up. He learned to dance the tango and other traditional dances. He was also a soccer fan. He especially liked the San Lorenzo de Almagro soccer club.

Jorge did well in school. He studied chemistry at the University of Buenos Aires. However, illness interrupted his studies. He got a serious lung infection when he was 21. Medicine was unavailable, so surgeons removed one of his lungs in 1957. Jorge recovered and continued his studies. After he graduated from the university, he worked in a laboratory. Still, Jorge felt a desire to live a life of service. At age 22, he decided to become a priest.

The San Lorenzo de Almagro Soccer Club

The San Lorenzo de Almagro soccer club is nicknamed "the Saints." It began in 1908 when a priest named Lorenzo Massa let a group of boys use church grounds for soccer. The team grew and gained many fans. Today the San Lorenzo club stadium has its own chapel. The stadium is located in a poor area of Buenos Aires. Pope Francis is still a fan of the club.

CHAPTER TWO

BEFORE HE WAS POPE

n 1958 Bergoglio began his training to become a Jesuit priest. The Jesuits are a community of priests and nonpriests called brothers. Bergoglio lived and studied in Argentina and nearby Chile while preparing for the priesthood. As part of his training, he served as a professor. He taught literature, religion, and other subjects to university students. In 1969 he was ordained a Jesuit priest.

Bergoglio spent years teaching and studying before he could become a priest.

During the Dirty War, army tanks rolled through the streets of Buenos Aires.

In the 1970s and 1980s, Bergoglio led churches and continued to study and teach. He studied in Spain and Germany, but he spent most of his career in Argentina. This was a difficult time in Argentina's history. In the late 1970s, part of the military took over the government. They ruled through fear and violence until 1983. That time is now known as the Dirty War. Thousands of Argentinians were kidnapped or killed. This included some priests accused of working against the government.

A Simple Leader

Many church leaders in Latin America respected Bergoglio. He was known for his service to others and his leadership. Because of this, he was given more and more responsibility. In 1992 Bergoglio became an auxiliary bishop in Buenos Aires. In this job, he assisted higher-ranking bishops. In 1998 he became the city's archbishop. This is the top local leader of the Catholic Church.

Even as he gained power, Bergoglio lived a simple life that matched his Jesuit philosophy. He could have lived in large houses. Instead he stayed in a small apartment. He traveled through Buenos Aires on buses and subways. He went out at night to sit

The Dirty War

During the Dirty War, the military used violence and fear to rule. They targeted people who disagreed with them. This included some Jesuit priests. The military did not target Bergoglio. However, they did target two priests who worked with him. Some critics have said Bergoglio did not do enough to defend people close to him. Supporters say he did as much as he could.

In 1998 Bergoglio, *right*, met Pope John Paul II, *left*, at the Vatican.

with homeless people on the street. He brought food to share with them. In his sermons, he taught about the importance of helping the poor. He also spoke of working together with people from all religions.

In 2001 he became a cardinal during an economic crisis in Argentina. He told church members not to attend the special Mass in Vatican City where he would be made a cardinal. Instead, he told people to give the money they would have spent traveling to the poor.

As a cardinal, Bergoglio was asked to make important decisions.

The Jesuits

The Jesuits are a community of Catholic priests and brothers. Saint Ignatius of Loyola founded the group in 1540. They are known for focusing on education and social justice. Jesuits study philosophy, theology, literature, and history. They also spend time teaching. It takes years of preparation to become a Jesuit priest. The Jesuits started many well-known universities. These include Georgetown University and Boston College, both in the United States. Pope Francis is the first Jesuit to become pope.

Pope Benedict XVI, *left*, met with Bergoglio, *right*, when Bergoglio was a cardinal.

In 2005 he traveled to Vatican City to help select a new pope. Some people thought Bergoglio might be elected pope at that time. Instead, Cardinal Joseph Ratzinger of Germany was selected. He became

Pope Benedict XVI. Bergoglio returned to Argentina. He planned to finish his work there. He wanted to retire in the country where he was born.

EXPLORE ONLINE

Chapter One and Chapter Two have lots of information about Bergoglio's life before he became pope. The website below has even more information about Bergoglio's life. As you know, every source is different. Reread the first two chapters of this book. What are the similarities between what you read here and the information you found on the website? Are there any differences? How do the two sources present information differently?

Pope Francis Biography
www.mycorelibrary.com/pope-francis

WHITE SMOKE

n early 2013, something unexpected happened.
Pope Benedict XVI decided that he could no
longer lead the church. He believed that the
effects of aging prevented him from carrying out
his role. This was surprising. Popes usually lead the
church until their deaths. Before Benedict XVI, they
almost never retired early. Once again, Bergoglio
traveled to Vatican City. This time he would do more

The resignation of Pope Benedict XVI gave Bergoglio a second
chance to become pope.

than just cast a vote. He would not leave the meeting to retire in Argentina. This time he would become Pope Francis.

Electing a Pope

Bergoglio was one of 115 cardinals who gathered in the Sistine Chapel in Vatican City in March 2013. They came from 50 countries. These 115 cardinals formed a papal conclave. This is a meeting to select the next pope. For hundreds of years, popes have been selected by papal conclaves.

The cardinals met, discussed, and voted for two days. To become pope, someone must get at least two-thirds of the votes plus one. All notes and ballots are burned after each vote.

The Sistine Chapel

The Sistine Chapel has been the site of papal conclaves and other important church functions for more than 500 years. It is older than its grand neighbor, Saint Peter's Basilica, where the pope holds Mass. The Sistine Chapel is filled with beautiful art. The most famous artwork is on the ceiling. The famous artist Michelangelo painted it in the early 1500s. The ceiling shows scenes from the first book of the Bible, Genesis.

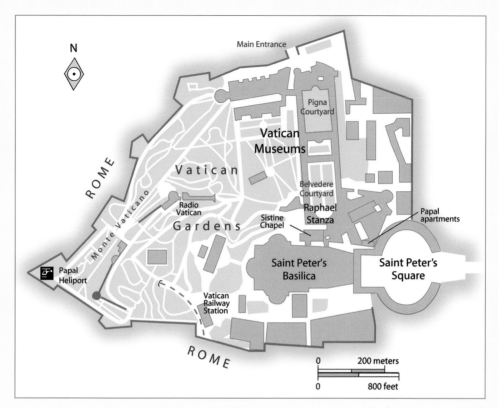

N

Main Entrance

Pigna Courtyard

Vatican Museums

ROME

Vatican

Monte Vaticano

Belvedere Courtyard

Radio Vatican

Raphael Stanza

Sistine Chapel

Gardens

Papal apartments

Papal Heliport

Saint Peter's Basilica

Saint Peter's Square

Vatican Railway Station

ROME

0   200 meters

0   800 feet

Vatican City Map

This is a map of Vatican City. Many of the places discussed in this book appear on this map. Can you remember what happens in the places marked on this map? Find where the papal conclave is held. Find where the crowds gathered to watch for the white smoke. Take a look at the map's scale. Does the size of Vatican City surprise you?

When no one receives the number of votes needed, black smoke appears from the chimney. This is a sign that no decision has been made. The cardinals then vote again.

Greeting the World

Bergoglio received enough votes to become pope on the second day of the conclave. White smoke poured from the chimney. Outside, the crowd celebrated. Inside, Bergoglio prepared to be introduced to the world as the new pope. When assistants brought him elaborate clothing to wear, he turned it down. He wanted to wear simple white clothes.

Then he chose a name. Bergoglio would now be called Pope

Francis, naming himself after Saint Francis of Assisi. At age 76, he would become the 266th pope in the history of the Catholic Church.

FURTHER EVIDENCE

Chapter Three has quite a bit of information about selecting a new pope. What is the main point of this chapter? What key evidence supports this point? Go to the article about the papal conclave at the website below. Find a quote from the website that supports the chapter's main point.

About the Papal Conclave
www.mycorelibrary.com/pope-francis

A NEW POPE

Pope Francis represents many firsts for the Catholic Church. He is the first pope from Latin America. He is the first Jesuit pope. He is the first pope to take the name of Francis. He is also the first to pope to dress in simple white clothes. People wondered what this new pope would do as leader of a big, powerful church.

Pope Francis's bedroom was plain and simple compared to the ornate palace used by previous popes.

The Pope's Clothes

The traditional clothes worn by the pope have changed little since the Middle Ages. At that time, church leaders wore clothing meant to show their power. In the past, popes wore a tall, folded hat called a miter. They also wore an elaborate cape called a mozzetta and red shoes.

Pope Francis dresses more simply. He wears a white ankle-length shirt called a cassock over plain black pants and shoes. Rather than a miter, he wears a basic white cap on his head.

In Vatican City, Pope Francis chose to live in a small apartment in a guesthouse instead of in the papal palace. Past popes were driven around in a special white car. Pope Francis has a simple blue sedan.

Tackling Problems

Pope Francis became leader of a church with difficult problems. Outsiders accused the Vatican of misusing money. And in Catholic churches around the world, there were cases of abuse. Priests who had hurt children had been allowed to continue working. There had been little punishment for their actions. These stories of abuse were kept secret for

We Will Not Be Silent

Turn Over Files!
Turn In Abusers!
Stop The Cover-Up!

Abuse scandals drew protests and harmed the reputation of the Catholic Church.

What Is Vatican City?

Vatican City is often simply called "the Vatican." Vatican City is a very small country that sits within Rome, Italy. It is the world's smallest nation. The Roman Catholic Church governs the Vatican.

Vatican City is surrounded by a wall. It contains important buildings, including Saint Peter's Basilica and the Sistine Chapel. It also possesses many famous works of art. In front of Saint Peter's Basilica is Saint Peter's Square. This large plaza is usually filled with tourists.

years. People suffered greatly because church leaders did not take the abuse cases seriously. As they learned about the abuse, some Catholics found it hard to trust the church.

Pope Francis asked eight cardinals to be his advisors. With their advice, he began dealing with the church's challenges. He gathered a group of experts to review cases of abuse. They also designed ways to protect children. Finally, the group changed the way money is handled at the Vatican.

Pope Francis gave many speeches. He also met with many world leaders in his new role. He gave a

Pope Francis met with world leaders whose social policies he disagreed with, including President Cristina Fernández of Argentina.

common message: do more for the poor and the suffering. While he did not change the church's beliefs, he told people not to judge one another. He asked that people be merciful to others. He told church leaders that simply giving money to the poor wasn't enough. It was also important to go out and be with people who are suffering.

Pope Francis, familiar with the severe poverty of Buenos Aires, made the poor a major focus of his work as pope.

Pope Francis's message connected with many people. However, some of his traditional Catholic views clashed with modern societies. For example, he criticized same-sex marriages, which have been long been frowned upon by the Catholic Church. Today, same-sex marriage is legal in many states and countries. This clash between Catholic teachings and modern viewpoints has caused many people to leave the church.

In one of his first official writings, Pope Francis expressed his vision for the work that the church should do. In this part of that document, he asks people to think more about those who live in poverty:

> *How can it be that it is not a news item when an elderly homeless person dies of exposure, but it is news when the stock market loses two points? This is a case of exclusion. Can we continue to stand by when food is thrown away while people are starving? This is a case of inequality. . . . Almost without being aware of it, we end up being incapable of feeling compassion at the outcry of the poor, weeping for other people's pain, and feeling a need to help them, as though all this were someone else's responsibility and not our own.*
>
> Source: Pope Francis. "Evangelii Gaudium: Apostolic Exhortation on the Proclamation of the Gospel in Today's World." Vatican. The Holy See, November 24, 2013. Web. Accessed April 28, 2014.

What's the Big Idea?

Take a close look at this statement. What is Pope Francis's main point about what is wrong in our world? Pick out two details he uses to make this point. What do you think Pope Francis hopes people will do after reading these words?

CHAPTER FIVE

THE WORLD WATCHES

Pope Francis's focus on the less fortunate and his simple lifestyle have attracted the attention and the respect of many people around the world. The "people's pope" is truly a newsmaker.

In 2013 he was named *Time* magazine's "Person of the Year." In 2014 he was named one of the "100 Most Influential People" in that same magazine.

The pope has attracted large crowds in his public appearances around the world.

US president Barack Obama contributed a short article about Pope Francis for that list. He wrote, "Rare is the leader who makes us want to be better people. Pope Francis is such a leader." Pope Francis appeared first on *Fortune* magazine's list of the world's greatest leaders. A fashion magazine even named him the "Best Dressed Man of 2013."

Meeting Leaders

Pope Francis met with many world leaders in the first few years after his election. His first meeting with President Obama came in March 2014. The president and the pope met at the Vatican. They gave each other gifts. Obama gave Pope Francis a box made of wood from the United

At their meeting, President Obama invited Pope Francis to visit the White House in Washington, DC.

States' first cathedral. The box contained a pouch of seeds. Pope Francis gave Obama two medallions. He also gave Obama a copy of a book he wrote about the poor.

The leaders posed for photos and met privately for an hour. They disagree on many issues, including same-sex marriage and abortion rights. Still, they were able to find common ground on the issue of poverty.

A Pope for the People

Some of the news about Pope Francis shows his playful side. He frequently poses for "selfies" with visitors to Vatican City.

Pilgrims in Saint Peter's Square

For centuries, people from all over the world have traveled to Saint Peter's Square. Some come for special blessings from the pope. Other travelers come to experience a beautiful and historic place. While Saint Peter's Square is especially full during special events, people fill the square throughout the year. Some visitors hope to see the pope during his weekly appearances. Others go to attend Mass at Saint Peter's Basilica.

Pope Francis's ability to engage with young and old people from around the world has made him one of the most popular popes in recent history.

He exchanged caps with college students. He gave two children a ride in the car he uses to drive through Saint Peter's Square.

Some stories show his kindness, such as when he stopped a weekly speech to hug a sick man who had traveled to see him. Other articles focus on how Pope Francis inspires people to do more for others. One article reported that approximately 25 percent of Catholics increased their donations to the poor in 2013. Many said Pope Francis was the reason they did so.

This pope from far away is making news and making a difference. He is a new pope in many ways. His kindness and simplicity have attracted the attention of the world.

On December 11, 2013, *Time* magazine named Pope Francis the "Person of the Year." The award is given each year to the one person who, in the editors' opinion, has been the year's most important newsmaker. Journalists Howard G. Chua-Eoan and Elizabeth Dias wrote why Pope Francis was given this honor:

> He took the name of a humble saint and then called for a church of healing. The first non-European pope in 1,200 years is poised to transform a place that measures change by the century. . . . But what makes this Pope so important is the speed with which he has captured the imaginations of millions who had given up on hoping for the church at all. . . . In a matter of months, Francis has elevated the healing mission of the church—the church as servant and comforter of hurting people in an often harsh world.
>
> Source: Howard Chua-Eoan and Elizabeth Dias. "Pope Francis, the People's Pope." Time. Time, December 11, 2013. Web. Accessed April 28, 2014.

Back It Up

The authors of this passage give examples to support a point. What is the point they are making? Write a paragraph describing it. Then, using what you have learned about Pope Francis, write two or three additional pieces of evidence to support this point.

IMPORTANT DATES

1936

Jorge Mario Bergoglio is born in Buenos Aires, Argentina.

1957

Bergoglio suffers a lung infection and has one lung removed.

1958

Bergoglio begins studying to become a Jesuit priest.

1998

Bergoglio becomes the Archbishop of Buenos Aires, the capital of Argentina.

2001

Bergoglio is named a cardinal at Vatican City in Rome.

2005

Bergoglio and other cardinals travel to Vatican City to select Pope Benedict XVI as the new pope.

1969

Bergoglio is ordained a Jesuit priest.

1970s–1980s

Bergoglio works as a priest during the Dirty War.

1992

Bergoglio becomes an auxiliary bishop.

2013

Bergoglio again travels with other cardinals to Vatican City to select a new pope in March.

2013

Bergoglio becomes Pope Francis on March 13.

2013

Pope Francis is named Time magazine's "Person of the Year."

Take a Stand

Popes have traditionally worn elaborate clothes and lived in fancy apartments. But Pope Francis has decided to continue living a simpler life that looks more like that of an ordinary person than a powerful leader. Do you think he should be living this way? Or should leaders live in a way that sets them apart from others? Write a short essay explaining your opinion. Make sure to give reasons for your opinion, and include facts and details that support those reasons.

Say What?

This story about the leader of a large and historic church includes many new vocabulary words. Find five words in this book that you've never heard before. Use a dictionary to find out what they mean. Then write the meanings in your own words, and use each word in a new sentence.

Tell the Tale

Chapter Three of this book discusses Pope Francis's election. Imagine you are watching from the conclave as the new pope is announced. Write 200 words telling the story of that night. Describe the sights and sounds of the room. How does Pope Francis react? Set the scene, develop a sequence of events, and offer a conclusion.

Dig Deeper

After reading this book, what questions do you still have about Pope Francis? With an adult's help, find a few reliable sources that can help you answer your questions. Write a paragraph about what you learned.

GLOSSARY

basilica
an important church

bishop
a high-ranking church leader in charge of a local area, called a diocese

cardinal
an important official, ranking just below the pope, in the Roman Catholic Church; all cardinals are also bishops

conclave
the meeting of the cardinals in charge of electing the new pope; the speeches and votes cast in the conclave are secret

Mass
a series of sacred prayers and ceremonies led by a priest in the Roman Catholic Church

ordain
to make a person a priest or a bishop in a special ceremony during Mass

papal
related to the pope

pilgrim
a person who travels to a holy place for religious reasons

sermon
a speech that gives religious instruction

theology
religious studies

LEARN MORE

Books

Kennedy, Robert F., Jr. *Saint Francis of Assisi: A Life of Joy*. New York: Disney–Hyperion, 2005.

Monge, M., J. S. Wolfe, and D. Kizlauskas. *Jorge from Argentina: The Story of Pope Francis for Children*. Boston, MA: Pauline Books & Media, 2013.

Websites

To learn more about Newsmakers, visit **booklinks.abdopublishing.com**. These links are routinely monitored and updated to provide the most current information available.

Visit **www.mycorelibrary.com** for free additional tools for teachers and students.

INDEX

ABOUT THE AUTHOR

Kris Woll is a writer and editor. She has a master's degree in history and lives with her family in Minneapolis, Minnesota.